Ancient Egyptian Children

Richard Tames
AR B.L.: 6.8
Points: 1.0

MG

Ancient Egyptian Children

Richard Tames

Heinemann Library
Chicago, Illinois

Customer Service 888-454-2279
Visit our website at www.heinemannlibrary.com

Design: Jo Hinton-Malivoire and Tinstar Design
Illustrations: Art Construction and Geoff Ward
Originated by Ambassador Litho
Printed in China by WKT Co.Ltd
07 06 05 04
10 9 8 7 6 5 4 3

Library of Congress Cataloging-in-Publication Data
Tames, Richard.
  Ancient Egyptian children / Richard Tames.
      p. cm. -- (People in the past)
Summary: Describes what life was like for children in ancient Egypt: what they ate, where they went to school, what games they played, and what they did at home.
Includes bibliographical references and index.
  ISBN 1-40340-309-0 (cased) -- ISBN 1-40340-513-1 (pbk.)
  1. Children--Egypt--History--Juvenile literature. 2. Children--Egypt--Social conditions--Juvenile literature. 3. Children--Egypt--Social life and customs--Juvenile literature. 4. Egypt--Civilization--To 332 B.C.--Juvenile literature. [1. Egypt--Civilization--To 332 B.C. 2. Egypt--Social life and customs.] I. Title. II. Series.
  HQ792.E19 T35 2003
  305.23'0932--dc21

                    2002012020

Acknowledgments
The author and publishers are grateful to the following for permission to reproduce copyright material: pp. 5, 24, 42 Phil Cooke/Magnet Harlequin; pp. 6, 9, 11, 16, 22, 26, 32, 36, 40, 41 AKG London; pp. 7, 30, 31 British Museum; pp. 8, 12, 18, 29 Michael Holford; pp. 10, 15, 17, 20, 28, 34, 43 Ancient Art and Architecture Collection; p. 14 C. M. Dixon; p. 38 Scala Art Library.

Cover photograph by AKG London.

Some words are shown in bold, **like this.** You can find out what they mean by looking in the glossary.

Contents

Land of the Pharaohs

▶ ◀▶ ◀▶ ◀▶ ◀▶ ◀▶ ◀▶ ◀▶ ◀▶ ◀▶ ◀▶ ◀▶ ◀▶ ◀▶ ◀▶ ◀▶ ◀

The amazing **civilization** of ancient Egypt was built along the banks of the Nile River. At 4,145 miles (6,670 kilometers), the Nile is the longest river in the world. Each year the melting of the snows in the mountains of Ethiopia caused the Nile to flood. Far away to the north in Egypt, the flooding river spread a layer of fertile black silt on the land for about 6 miles (10 kilometers) on either side. This narrow strip widened to 155 miles (250 kilometers) in the **delta** where the river split into many channels as it made its way into the Mediterranean Sea.

Civilization by the Nile

The annual flooding of the Nile renewed the fertility of the fields. The river provided the Egyptians with ducks, geese, and fish for food. It also aided the growth of **flax** to be made into **linen** cloth, and reeds and **papyrus** for writing on and making into boats, baskets, and sandals. The Nile also served as the country's main transportation system. The river made it possible to move around the huge quantities of stone needed to build the massive pyramid tombs of the pharaohs who ruled the land. The ancient-Greek **historian** Herodotus called ancient Egypt "The Gift of the Nile" because the riches of the river made the country great.

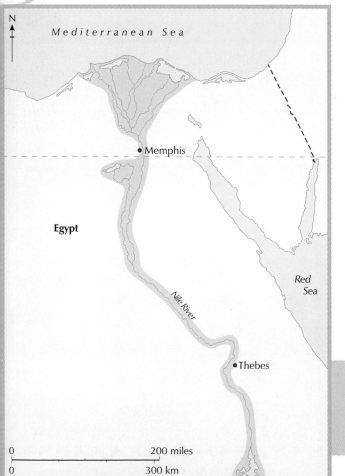

This map shows the course of the River Nile as it runs through Egypt toward the Mediterranean Sea.

The Colossi of Memnon is the name given to these gigantic stone statues. Although damaged by wind, sand, and frost, they have survived the last 3,350 years. They were built under the instruction of Pharaoh Amenhotep III.

Egypt was rich in **copper** that could be made into tools, and in gold that could be made into jewelry and traded. There was abundant stone for building temples and tombs, and flint for making into knives, sickles for cutting wheat and reeds, and war clubs. Timber for making boats and furniture was scarce, and much had to be bought in from other countries.

The people of Egypt

Thanks to its rich resources ancient Egypt was able to support a population of up to 5 million people, and to create a civilization that lasted for over 3,000 years. The Egyptians often lived short lives and many children died when they were still young. This book looks at the evidence that survives to tell us about the children of ancient Egypt, and explores what it can tell us about their lives.

Black land and red land

The Egyptians named their country after the color of its rich soil. They called their country *Kemet*, which means the "black land." They believed the color black was good or lucky. On either side of the Nile valley there was hot, windy *Deshret*, the desert or "red land." The Egyptians believed only the dead lived there. Red was therefore a bad and unlucky color. Desert made up nine-tenths of Egypt's territory and served as a barrier against foreign invaders. Most of Egypt's people lived around the river—on the black land.

Invisible Children

Historians try to rebuild the past out of what people made or wrote. Most of what the Egyptians made is lost forever. Items made of the most common materials—wood or wax, clay or cloth, bone or leather—are most likely to be broken, burned, or decomposed. The same is true of **papyrus** or parchment documents.

What has survived tells us much less about children than it does about adults. Children had far fewer possessions than adults, and what they did have was not made to last. Adult possessions, including tools, weapons, or jewelry were made of stone or metal, and were much more likely to survive. Children could not write about their lives, as adults did. Most never learned to write, and those that did were no longer children by the time they could write.

Surviving evidence

Despite these problems a huge amount of evidence has survived thanks to two particular features of ancient-Egyptian **civilization.** Egypt's hot, dry climate has preserved many items that would have decayed in a damp country. Also the Egyptians' firm belief in the **afterlife** led them to **mummify** bodies, bury them with their possessions, and decorate their tombs with elaborate paintings and **inscriptions.** Some of these tombs have survived.

This stone sculpture is a portrait of one of the daughters of Pharaoh Akenaten. Very little evidence of ancient-Egyptian children survives.

Records of poor children are rare. In this painting the artist showed poor boys helping with the grain harvest.

Children's tombs often contain favorite dolls, toys, and feeding bottles. They also have inscriptions which show how sad their parents were that they died. Their skeletons sometimes show signs of accidents. Modern science can also tell from their bones and teeth how well they were fed, and whether they had any serious illnesses.

The rich and the poor

As with other ancient civilizations, we know far more about the lives of the few rich and powerful people than we do about the lives of the ordinary farmers, who were most of the population. The rich owned more possessions, and were more likely to be able to write or be written about. They could afford expensive burials, even for their children. Ordinary Egyptians could not. Most of what we know of the lives of ordinary people comes from the viewpoint of the people they worked for.

Brief lives

If we could add up the lives of all the people who ever lived in ancient Egypt the children would outnumber the adults. Ancient Egyptians did not have as many doctors and medicines as we do and life could be hard. Many children died before they were old enough to have children of their own. But we know much more about the lives of adults than of children.

Having Children

"A man with many children is happy because people think well of him because he has them."

Egyptians wanted large families, as this advice from a scribe shows. The Pharaoh Ramses II is said to have had about 45 sons and about 40 daughters with his 7 wives. Wives were expected to have one baby after another. A wife unable to have children thought she was cursed by the gods. Other women pitied her.

Giving birth

When a woman had a baby she was normally helped by nurses and **midwives.** In ordinary families, these helpers would often have been members of the mother's own family. Egyptian women gave birth in a shelter made of poles and branches, roofed with reed mats. This was built on the roof of their house or in its courtyard or garden. They stayed there for fourteen days after the birth. This would have allowed them to give the new baby their full attention, and helped the mother relax and not worry about the rest of the family. It may also have helped to cut down the risk of infection because the mother and child were separated from other members of the household at a time when both baby and mother were most likely to catch something.

Ivory wands such as this one were thought to protect their owners. Pregnant women used them as charms to help them survive childbirth, and keep both the mother and child healthy.

8

A dangerous time

Childbirth was very risky. Having babies too soon greatly increased the chances that either the mother or the baby would die. Repeated childbirth often weakened mothers and increased the danger of later births. Egyptians believed that Seshat, the goddess of writing and arithmetic, decided at the moment of their birth how long a person would live. If a baby died when, or soon after, it was born it may have been thrown to the crocodiles, or left at the edge of the desert for hyenas to eat. Older babies who died might be buried under the house, wrapped in palm leaves or **linen.** Although some had food, lucky charms, necklaces, or toys buried with them, they were rarely **mummified** in the same way as adults.

About half of all mothers died by the age of 40, although they would have had children at a young age. Because husbands were often older than their wives, few men lived long enough to know their grandchildren.

The decoration and shape of this jug show a kneeling mother hugging her baby to her. Most ancient Egyptian mothers would have had many babies.

Looking after mother and child

Women prayed to the goddess Taweret who brought babies to the childless. This goddess looked like a pregnant hippopotamus with the arms and legs of a lion, and the back and tail of a crocodile. Beds were often painted with pictures of Taweret and babies' bottles were made in her shape.

Caring for Children

The high rate of deaths among babies and small children made Egyptian parents anxious to protect them in any way they could. They made charms from garlic, honey, and river fish. They said prayers every morning as they tied a protective **amulet** around the child's arm or neck. Babies were also kept close to their mothers, either being carried on her hip, or in a **linen** sling on her back. It seems likely that most ancient Egyptian mothers had as many as eight or nine babies, but three or four of these babies probably died before they turned five years old.

Babies were usually breast-fed until they were three. Breast-feeding was safer than eating regular food because the baby was less likely to come into contact with germs. Evidence suggests that when Egyptian infants started to eat solid food at the age of three, their death-rate rose sharply as a result of stomach infections.

This woman holds a child in a sling as she picks fruit in the garden. It was common for babies to be strapped to their mother or nurse in this way.

Pharaoh Akhenaten and his wife Nefertiti sit with their three daughters. The young children to the right are shown with shaved heads and the central girl has a **sidelock**.

Wet nurses

The wives of pharaohs and other wealthy men did not breast-feed their babies themselves. Instead they hired **wet nurses** to do this for them. Wet nurses were paid in goods such as necklaces, combs, sandals, baskets, and cooking oil.

The wet nurse of a pharaoh's child might be the wife of a general or some high official, and she was treated with great honor. Paintings of royal people often include their wet nurse. Sometimes the wet nurse was kept on as a nanny. When royal infants grew up they usually thought of the children of their wet nurse as being like their own brothers and sisters. The royal family would help these people get good jobs and marry well.

Naming the child

A baby was named immediately after birth in case it died soon afterward. This explains names such as "Welcome to you," "She belongs to me," "It is our sister," "This boy I wanted," and "The pretty girl has joined us." There is a woman's name, "Beni," that literally means "Sweetie." Most names would have referred to a god or goddess. Daughters were often given the same name as their mother. For this reason many also had a nickname to make clear who was who. Babies might also be named after a member of the royal family.

Home Life

Most Egyptians lived in villages near the river. Children played close to home to avoid the crocodiles and hippos that lived along the banks of the river. Snakes and scorpions were common in the desert. Most homes were single-story houses built of bricks. Bricks were made by mixing sticky river mud with chopped-up straw. Children could help pack this mixture into wooden molds and take the bricks out after they had dried in the sun.

The entrance to the home was also the family chapel, with offerings, like models of Egypt's gods, and busts of **ancestors.** The main room usually had an earthenware bench around the walls, for sitting and sleeping on. There were smaller sleeping and storage rooms off this. Cooking and messy jobs were done out in the courtyard, a safe area for infants to play in. The toilet was a stool over a sand-pit. Thick walls kept houses cool, and also provided room for niches to store or display things. In hot weather the whole family slept on reed mats on the flat roof.

This clay model of an ancient Egyptian house shows the area in front of the home where children would have played.

Drinking beer

Children and adults drank beer made from barley. It was thick and sweetened with spices, dates, or honey. One tomb painting shows a child with a bowl and has writing saying, "Give me some beer because I am hungry."

Rich people's homes had wall-torches or lamps to give light. There was not much furniture. The main items were wooden-framed beds, folding or fixed stools, low tables, and chests for storage. Wealthy homes had gardens with flowers, fruit, vegetables, herbs, trees for shade, and a pool for fish and for watering the plants. Children would have spent much of their time outside.

Food and drink

Both rich and poor Egyptians lived mainly on bread, fish, and vegetables, often made into stews, soups, or porridge. **Archaeologists** have found remains of over 40 different kinds of bread, cake, and cookie. Some were flavored with salt, honey, spices, or fruit. Some had a hole that could be filled with an egg or with beans.

The poor ate only at sunrise and dusk. The rich sometimes ate in the afternoon as well. Bread flour was often coarsely ground with pieces of stone or sand left in it. As a result, even children as young as ten might have badly worn teeth. A mixture of honey and herbs was used to soothe a toothache. Poor children ate meat only at religious festivals or family celebrations. The children of the rich ate meat often. Poor children ate dates as their sweetener, while the wealthy used honey.

Clothes and Fashions

▶◀▶◀▶◀▶◀▶◀▶◀▶◀▶◀▶◀▶◀▶◀▶◀▶◀▶◀▶◀▶◀

Egyptian paintings usually show children naked. Most children probably were naked in summer, but not all the time. Artists showed them naked to make it clear they were children, and to distinguish them from adults. Children can also be identified by their hairstyle—the head shaved, with a piece of hair hanging down as a **sidelock.** Shaving the head prevented head lice.

From the age of about twelve children were expected to wear some clothes all the time, during the summer and winter. The world's oldest surviving garment is a pleated **linen** shirt made for an Egyptian child around 2800 B.C.E., and now in a museum in Oxford, England. It had detachable sleeves to be sewn on for cold weather. Men wore a short **kilt** that was knotted or buckled at the waist. Women wore **tunics** and in paintings they are shown in tube dresses with either one or two shoulder straps. Laborers just wore a **loincloth.** Cloaks, shawls, tunics, and furs were worn in winter.

Ancient Egyptian people liked to arrange children's hair into a sidelock. The child shown sitting on the adult's lap has her hair arranged in this way.

Linen clothes

Most people wore linen clothes that were made at home. Most children's clothes would have been made by their mothers. Linen was light, cool, and easy to wash and dry in the hot sun. Making linen took a long time, but the early stages were simple enough that older children could help with them. **Flax** plants were gathered by hand, tied in bundles, dried out, combed to take out the seed capsules, and soaked in water to separate the fibers. These were beaten to soften them, washed, and then spun into yarn. The yarn was woven into cloth. Linen was difficult to dye, so most garments were left plain.

Children and poorer people often went barefoot. Wealthier people wore sandals made of leather or woven reed or grass. Children and men, as well as women, wore jewelry. They also wore **amulets,** which were charms to protect them.

Royal children

Members of the royal family were expected to look as amazing as the gods. The tomb of the boy pharaoh Tutankhamen was stuffed with clothes, including over 50 shirts and shawls, 30 gloves, and over 100 triangular loincloths. There were also caps, belts, scarves, and sandals. A baby's robe that was found in the tomb was made of linen so fine it must have taken over 3,000 hours to make.

This painting of the dead man and his family was found in the tomb of the workman Inkerhau. The adults wear white linen clothes. The children are shown naked but they are wearing some pieces of jewelry.

Family Life

The ancient Egyptians believed that death was only an interruption of life and not the end of it. They thought of the family as consisting of dead relatives as well as the living. Even the poorest homes often had statues of **ancestors** on display. They were a constant reminder to children of family members they were too young to have known, but who were still watching what they did from the **afterlife.** Tomb paintings can mislead us into thinking that Egyptian households normally had many children because they show the children who died as well as those who lived.

Children were valued because they would look after their parents in old age, when they were too feeble to look after themselves. It was just as important to the Egyptians that their children should continue to look after them when they were dead. This meant making sure that their parents' tombs were built and that they were buried according to Egyptian customs.

Egyptian families preferred to have boy babies. All children were thought of as a blessing. However, boys were preferred because they were responsible for taking care of their aging parents. They could also be heads of their own households when they grew up.

This sculpture was made in about 1550 B.C.E. By showing this family group with their arms around each other, the artist suggests they were close and loving.

Adopted sons and daughters

A married couple who were unable to have children of their own, or whose children had all died would try to adopt one. This would make sure that there would be someone to arrange their funerals, inherit their property, take over the man's job, and bring offerings to their tombs.

Arranging funerals

The eldest son played an important part in his parents' funerals. When people wrote a **will,** it often said that their surviving children had to pay for their funeral before they could inherit anything. A dead person could only enter the afterlife if funeral ceremonies had been performed properly. Once they had entered the afterlife the dead needed their surviving relatives to bring offerings of food and drink to their tombs to allow their souls to live on.

Girls were married to the sons of other families and this meant they were not there to look after their own aging parents. It made sense to make sure daughters got married as soon as possible because the older they got the more they cost to feed and dress. Most girls were married by the time they were 14. It was thought men should marry by the age of 20. Many cousins married each other. Often, men married their nieces.

This sculpture shows Seneb with his wife, Senetites, and their two children. The children have been made to look much smaller than the adults and have fingers in their mouths. Artists often exaggerated the small size of children.

Working at Home

▶ ◀▶ ◀▶ ◀▶ ◀▶ ◀▶ ◀▶ ◀▶ ◀▶ ◀▶ ◀▶ ◀▶ ◀▶ ◀▶ ◀▶ ◀▶ ◀▶ ◀▶ ◀▶ ◀

Wealthy people had **slaves** to do all their household work, so the children of rich parents did not have to help out around the home. Most children did do some work from about the age of five. They began by taking care of their younger brothers and sisters, running errands, and fetching water from the river or from a nearby well. They also helped with sweeping and with carrying food out to people working in the fields of their village.

The harvesting of crops was a very important part of ancient-Egyptian life. Much food needed to be grown to keep everyone fed. Children picked up grain that was dropped by the men who carried it from the fields to a threshing floor. They would take the grain home for their families. Oxen would walk over the crops collected by the men to separate the stalks from the ears.

In Egyptian art, women are normally shown as paler than the men because they were expected to spend more time indoors, out of the fierce sunlight. Baking bread and brewing beer were done daily because neither would keep for long. Girls would learn how to do these essential chores by helping their mothers. As they got older they would master the other main job women did, making **linen** and weaving it into cloth. Basket-weaving was another important skill. Grasses, **papyrus,** and palm leaves were all used to make baskets and chests for storing food and clothes. They were also used to make mats for floor coverings and roofing. Herbs were grown close to the house for use in cooking and making medicines.

Working in the fields

Farm work was the most common way of making a living. Tomb paintings often show children helping. In the spring, young boys helped to clean out **irrigation ditches** and drive the livestock across the fields to stomp in the seeds. Children also helped to scare away birds from eating the growing crops by shouting and throwing stones. They also had curved sticks, like boomerangs, which were thrown at birds in flight to bring them down. After the harvest children searched the fields, picking up fallen scraps of grain. Because wood was very scarce, it was expensive to burn. Children were sent to gather animal droppings that were dried out in the sun to be used for fuel.

The sons of craftsmen or artists followed in their father's trade. Because so much of Egypt was desert, there was a shortage of timber. This meant that furniture-makers learned how to disguise poor quality wood by covering it with ebony or ivory. Glassmakers also recycled broken items to turn them into **amulets,** beads, or containers for makeup. While it is common for paintings of farm work to show children helping out, they are not included in pictures showing craftsmen at work.

Working away from Home

▶◀▶◀▶◀▶◀▶◀▶◀▶◀▶◀▶◀▶◀▶◀▶◀▶◀▶◀▶◀▶◀▶◀

Many Egyptian farmers were **serfs,** tied by law to the land of their village—which provided them with work and food. A farmer's daughters were more likely than his sons to leave their village. They usually left to get married, although there were some jobs open to females—servant, **weaver,** baker, musician, dancer, **wet nurse,** and laundry worker.

The sons of craftsmen would normally learn their father's trade.

Egyptian ideas about work

This saying from the **New Kingdom** period tells us what the Egyptians thought about children working: "You shall not spare your body when you are young; food comes about by the hands, provision by the feet." This means that children had to work hard if they wanted to eat.

If a craftsman had several sons they might all learn his trade, but some might need to move to a city to find work. Boys who wanted to be soldiers went to work in a **fort,** an army post used for defense. They began by helping **grooms** look after **chariot** horses, and cleaning soldiers' weapons and equipment.

Servants

Rich families in ancient Egypt often employed servants. They would have worked in the kitchen and around the house. Many of these servants would have been young people who had been sent out to earn money because their families could not afford to support them. Girls would probably have married when they were in their early teens. Those who were not married often left home to work as maids for wealthy women. They would have lived on the estates where they worked, and would have seen their own families only rarely, if at all.

Slavery

Slaves were not as common in ancient Egypt as they were in ancient Greece or Rome. Most were foreigners, Nubians from the south, or people from the Near East. Slaves were usually either captured as prisoners of war, or were the children of people who had been captured or bought from slave traders. Slave traders either bought or kidnapped people in their home countries. Some people sold themselves and their children into slavery because it was the only way they could pay off their debts.

School

The Egyptian system of writing with **hieroglyphs** took many years to learn. At most only one or two children in every hundred learned to read and write well. Being literate, or able to read and write, was essential to a job as a government official, army officer, scribe, or priest. The importance of literacy in ancient Egypt can be seen from the many surviving statues that show a person with writing equipment.

This statue shows a young man in the typical pose of a scribe. He pulls his **kilt** tight across his legs so that he has a surface to support his papyrus. Young scribes practiced writing on boards, but experienced scribes wrote on papyrus scrolls. Scribes were also taught to do arithmetic, so that they could work out taxes.

Advice for scribes

Schooling was not meant to be enjoyable. The scribe Amenemope warned his son, "pass no day in idleness or you will be beaten. The ear of a boy is on his back. He listens when he is beaten." He also told his son why it was worth putting up with school, "No scribe is short of food and of riches from the palace." Scribes did not pay taxes or have to work on building projects either. The alternatives were much worse:"I have seen the smith at work at the opening of his furnace … he stinks more than fish roe … the potter … grubs in the mud more than a pig."

There was a school attached to the royal court where the pharaoh's children were taught. Sometimes this might include girls as well, though normally only boys went to school. Other pupils at the court school would be children of foreign rulers whose countries were under Egyptian control, and children of the pharaoh's generals, officials, and priests. Some children from ordinary families might also be sent there. Being at school with a future pharaoh gave these children the chance of a career in his government. Some temples also had schools, although there were no special school buildings. Classes were held in the open air.

Learning from books

Lessons were based on written textbooks that did not change for centuries. These books were not like our books—they were in fact long scrolls made up of several sheets of **papyrus.** Pupils were not expected to understand what they were writing until they were older. Learning things by heart was a very important skill, and so was learning to speak clearly and confidently. A man's speech could earn him favors. Egyptian boys were taught to keep calm at all times, and to think before saying or doing anything.

Reading and Writing

▶◀▶ ◀▶ ◀▶ ◀▶ ◀▶ ◀▶ ◀▶ ◀▶ ◀▶ ◀▶ ◀▶ ◀▶ ◀▶ ◀▶ ◀▶ ◀◀

Papyrus was expensive so Egyptian children learned to write by practicing on broken bits of pottery, which the Greeks called *ostraca*. *Ostraca* found at the workmen's village at Deir el-Medina show they were also used for everyday notes between neighbors. This means that skilled working men—and sometimes even their wives too—could read and write a little. The son of a scribe, however, would master a whole range of standard documents and letters that he would have to write many times over in the course of his career.

Pictures and signs made up hieroglyphs. Although records were kept on papyrus, colorful hieroglyphs were written on walls. They were a sacred form of writing. Here, among other signs, owls, snakes, and eyes are used to make words.

Papyrus—the first paper

Most writing was done on papyrus. This was a paper made from a reed that grew along the banks of the River Nile. Separate sheets of papyrus were stuck together in long rolls. The longest sheet to have survived dates from around 1150 B.C.E., and measures about 45 yards (41 meters). Papyrus lasted for centuries as long as it did not get damp.

Hieroglyphs

The most formal style of writing was known as *medu netjer,* which means "divine words." The Greeks translated this term as **hieroglyph,** meaning "sacred writing." Hieroglyphs were used on monuments and tombs. There were over 6,000 hieroglyphs, though only a few hundred were in common use.

Some hieroglyphs were simplified pictures of what they referred to, such as a man or a loaf of bread. Others were pictures standing for sounds. A picture of a human foot represented the sound "b." All sound signs stood for consonants. There were no signs for vowels, which the reader guessed about on their own. Hieroglyphs could be written side to side or top to bottom. The oldest known hieroglyphic writing dates back to around 3200 B.C.E. The last known hieroglyphic **inscription** dates from C.E. 394.

In addition to hieroglyphs there was a simpler script, known as **hieratic,** which read from right to left—the opposite of the way you are reading this page. Hieratic could be written quickly, and was used for most daily purposes, especially writing documents

The main writing instrument was a reed, cut at the end to make a nib, or point. Ink was made out of vegetable gum and soot. Scribes carried their pens and inks in special boxes.

Math and Measurements

Unlike the ancient Greeks, the Egyptians did not spend a lot of time on mathematics that could not be used for measurement and other useful things. The dimensions of the pyramids show that they could measure distances and quantities with astonishing accuracy. The sides of the largest pyramid are 251 yards (230 meters) long, and differ from each other by only a few inches.

Practical Problems

Boy scribes probably only began to learn mathematics near the end of their training. One use was for recording the taxes they collected. Another was working out how much they should collect next season. They did this by using knotted ropes to measure the area of land being farmed. They then used the "Nilometer," marked scales at different points along the Nile, to calculate the river's height, and estimate the strength of its annual flooding.

These two measurements enabled them to work out roughly how much food would be grown in an area, and therefore how much could be taken in taxes. A surviving mathematical text also shows how to work out how much grain a granary could hold.

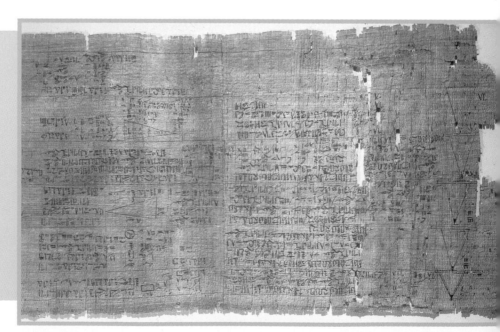

This mathematical **papyrus** is called Papyrus Rhind. Calculations on it were used to work out how much grain could be fitted into a granary. On part of it, the scribe has divided some of the grain into fractions.

Different signs mean different amounts. The signs were put together to make larger numbers.

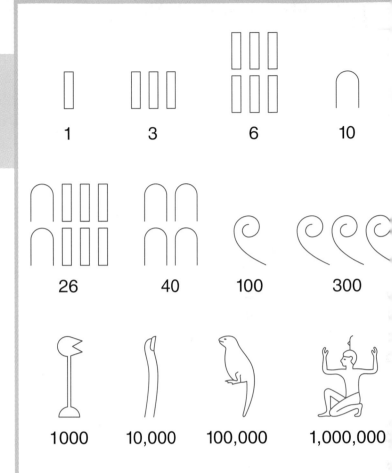

1 3 6 10

26 40 100 300

1000 10,000 100,000 1,000,000

Measuring

The Egyptians used the "cubit" as their standard unit of measurement. The cubit was based on the length of a man's forearm, and would have been equal to 20 3/8 inches (52.4 centimeters.) The cubit was subdivided into seven palm-widths. Each palm-width equaled four thumb-widths.

Time

Most children had no need to tell the time accurately. They simply got up when it was light, and went to bed when it was dark. Those who did need to tell time used water-clocks. These were containers with sticks that showed how much water had flowed out of the vessel and therefore how much time had passed.

Counting money?

Children did not need to know how to count money. Egyptians had no coins to use as money, but they did use weights of **copper** to calculate the value of different items. This made it easier to work out how many woven baskets one should barter, or trade, for a jar of oil. Wages and taxes were usually paid in goods or produce such as barley, honey, **linen,** or reed mats.

Toys

It is not easy to be certain that what looks like an ancient-Egyptian toy actually is a toy. What look to us like dolls or puppets were often used for religious purposes, such as an offering to the gods. Many tombs contain *shabtis*, carved and painted wooden figures. These figures were meant to work as servants for the dead person in the **afterlife.** What look like toy boats and model houses or farms have also been found in the tombs of adults. These were clearly not toys, but examples of what the adults would find or need in the afterlife.

Most children's toys were easily broken or destroyed over time by dampness or fire, so few have survived. Some have been found intact in the tombs of young children. Others are illustrated in paintings. Family members made most toys. Children in rich families might have toys made by skilled craftsmen.

Toys for babies

Babies were given rattles made of dried wood or gourds (a type of plant), clay pottery, or bone. Some had metal bells or loose pebbles inside. Figures of farmyard or pet animals were made out of clay, wood, or **bronze.** Dolls were made out of cloth and wax. They often had movable arms and legs and different sets of clothes for dressing up. Some dolls have been found with holes drilled into their scalp to hold "hair" made from fibers of **flax.**

This painted wooden toy horse and this pottery horse would have been the toys of children living in Egypt under Roman rule. They are just under 2,000 years old.

Older children played with tops. These were usually made of wood, but some were made of clay and covered by faience—a glass-like glaze. These would have been expensive to make. However, the faience tops were very pretty and would last much longer than wooden ones, as well as spinning better. Another luxury toy that was found in Egypt consists of a base that has little ivory figures on it. The figures twirl around when a string is pulled.

Children in ancient Egypt would have played with toys like these. A glaze on the doll makes her look turquoise. The cat has moveable jaws and bronze teeth. They were made in about 1450 B.C.E. and 1300 B.C.E.

Children and pets

The problem of knowing what was a toy also applies to pets because birds and animals were also offered to the gods. Egyptian children kept cats, dogs, and monkeys as pets as well as different kinds of birds such as pigeons, ducks, and other birds found near the river. However, pictures showing children with geese or gazelles are probably not showing them as pets. Geese can harm small children, and gazelles cannot be tamed.

Games and Sports

▶◀▶ ◀▶ ◀▶ ◀▶ ◀▶ ◀▶ ◀▶ ◀▶ ◀▶ ◀▶ ◀▶ ◀▶ ◀▶ ◀▶ ◀▶ ◀

Children could go swimming in **irrigation canals** and ride on donkeys. Although most fishing was done with nets or traps, some was done by harpooning. This way of fishing was less certain of success but more exciting.

Ball games

Children played many games with balls made in different ways. The outer covering might be cloth, leather, or **papyrus,** and the stuffing inside could be barley husks, straw, grass, rags, reeds, or horsehair. Wooden balls were used to knock down pins as in bowling. Some games were played by rolling the balls through gaps in a gateway before they hit the pins. Girls favored juggling, usually with three balls. The best could juggle while keeping their arms crossed. There were also girls' games that involved throwing and catching balls while clapping in between throws and catches.

The British Museum owns these rare ancient-Egyptian toys. Balls were used in many kinds of games.

Egyptian paintings rarely show boys and girls playing together. Boys' games were sometimes rough. One, called "jumping over the goose," needed two boys to sit facing each other with arms clasped together to make a barrier. As other boys jumped over their arms, they tried to catch a trailing foot to bring the jumper crashing down. Arm-wrestling and leap-frog were also popular. Most games were played by two, or only a few players. Tug-of-war was one of the few team games. To toughen them up for the army older boys did sports such as wrestling, fighting with the **quarterstaff,** and target-shooting with a bow and arrows.

Senet

Both rich and poor children, and adults, played board games. The exact rules for their use are not known. The most popular game was "Senet" ("passing"), that seems to have been like a complicated form of chutes and ladders. Each player usually had seven pieces that had to be moved along a grid of three rows of ten squares. Some of the squares were lucky and others were unlucky. Moves were decided by throwing sets of animal knuckle-bones that were used the way we use dice. One Senet board, from the tomb of Tutankhamen, was made in the shape of a box, with a playing surface on top that was inlaid with ivory. The ivory playing-pieces and knuckle-bones used in the game were stored inside. The game could be played much more simply by scratching a board on stone or even in sand or dust, and using pebbles for counters.

Sickness and Health

The death rate among babies and small children in ancient Egypt was very high. Infants often died from **dysentery,** a stomach infection caused by poor hygiene, such as drinking dirty water or eating unwashed fruit and vegetables. When there was no obvious cause for illness, like a wound or insect bite, the sickness was blamed on evil spirits. A child's parents would sometimes make a medicine to keep harmful spirits away. One medicine was described this way: "I have prepared a potion ... made from a poisonous herb, from garlic ... and honey ... ."

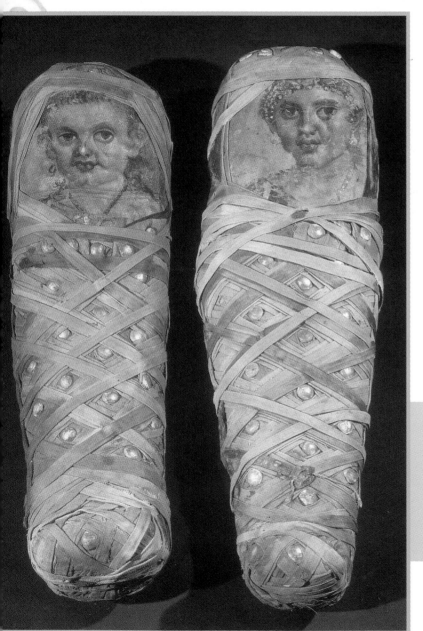

There are few surviving mummies of children, but some have been found. As with adult mummies, they are the bodies of children from rich and influential families.

Clues from mummies

Mummifying so many bodies must have improved the Egyptians' knowledge of human **anatomy,** or how the body works. It certainly helps modern **archaeologists** find out what kinds of diseases young Egyptians had. Many suffered from lung diseases caused by the hot and dusty climate in which they lived.

Mothers also tried to protect their babies by tying written spells around their necks. These spells were supposed to ward off diseases and accidents. Bites from snakes and scorpions were a common danger because children often walked around in bare feet. Cuts or burns that became poisoned could also lead to early death. Mothers were advised that a child with teething troubles should be fed a fried mouse.

Short lives

There are 26 royal **mummies** in the Egyptian Museum at Cairo. Because they were better fed and cared for, and less exposed to danger or fatigue than any other group, the royal family should have had the best chances for a long life. However, X-rays show that only Pharaoh Ramses II lived past the age of 55. Three more members of the royal family died between the ages of 40 and 50. All the rest died between the ages of 20 and 40. The bodies of nearly 300 ordinary people, dug up from a cemetery at Abusir, showed that their average age at death was between nineteen and twenty.

Egyptian doctors could mend broken bones with splints, and knew how to heal bad cuts with bandages and special wrappings made from bread and herbs called **poultices.** Along with these practical skills, they often used lucky charms and spells as part of their treatment. Poor children would probably not have been able to afford to see a doctor. They would have relied on their parents' herbal remedies to keep them healthy.

Beliefs and Behavior

▶◀▶◀▶◀▶◀▶◀▶◀▶◀▶◀▶◀▶◀▶◀▶◀▶◀▶◀▶◀▶◀▶

Although ancient Egypt was a rich land where people could live well, it also suffered from droughts, **epidemics,** and invasions. It was normal for people to see many of their children die young. Perhaps for these reasons the Egyptians believed that the world ought to be unchanging and orderly. The goddess Maat, goddess of truth and justice, represented the idea of order. She also controlled the regular pattern of the stars and seasons. The task of the pharaoh was to rule as the servant of Maat. He did this by performing religious ceremonies to keep the gods in touch with the people. He also punished thieves, and defended Egypt against invaders.

Over the course of more than 3,000 years Egypt was governed by 30 different **dynasties** of pharaohs. Peaceful rule was interrupted by wars, disasters, and periods of disorder. Each time the Egyptians would rebuild their way of life under a new ruler on

A glazed hippopotamus statue of the goddess Taweret. She was the goddess of childbirth. The statue was made in about 400 B.C.E.

34

Advice for sons

This advice for the boys has been found:

"If a man's son accepts his father's words, his plans will not fail ... When he is old and respected he will speak likewise to his own children, renewing the teaching of his father ... he will speak to his children so that they in turn will speak to their children. Set an example ... if Maat is upheld then your children will live ... a dutiful son is a gift from heaven."

what they believed to be the same traditional ways. Children were therefore brought up to follow the customs of the past. These would teach them how to behave correctly toward other family members, neighbors, guests, strangers, priests, and officials of the pharaoh.

Winning favor

Boys were often named after their uncle or grandfather because he was a good person they should copy. Boys were brought up to believe that the greatest good fortune was to win royal favor by serving bravely as a soldier or working hard as a scribe. The pharaoh's closest servants were known as the "king's sons" even when they were not related to him at all. A successful career meant a man would receive a pleasant home and a good reputation. It also meant being able to look forward to being reborn in the **afterlife.**

Girls were brought up to be obedient, hard-working, and silent. They should want to devote their life to their husband, and have many children. The goddess Isis was held up as the ideal wife and mother every girl should want to grow up to be.

Holidays and Festivals

The craftsmen who lived in the village of Deir el-Medina worked eight days out of every week of ten days. There were also between 50 and 75 public festivals a year, some lasting several days. This gave the craftsmen time off to do other things, such as hunting and fishing. They might take their older sons with them to teach them how to use a throwing-stick, or fish with a net.

Hunters scare birds into flight in this tomb scene. The man and child on the left both have throwing-sticks to use on the birds. Holidays were popular times for hunting and fishing.

Horus as a child

The same god could take different forms and have different names. The important god Horus could be shown as a falcon, or as a man with a falcon's head. He could also be shown as a child standing on a crocodile surrounded by snakes, scorpions, and other dangerous animals. Showing him as a child with a **sidelock** was a way of reminding people he was the child of Isis.

When shown as a child Horus was known as Hor-Pa-Khered, or Harpocrates. An **amulet** with Harpocrates on it was supposed to protect the wearer from snake bites or scorpion stings.

Preparing for festivals

Festivals were held to honor the gods. Normally only priests were allowed to go inside temples at festival times, so the statues of gods were brought out. They were paraded around for all to see and ask favors from. Some were carried on portable **shrines,** others floated in specially built boats.

At various points in Egyptian cities and towns special stands were built and decorated, so that statues of the gods could rest and be seen by the people of that neighborhood. Before a big festival took place there would be days of preparation. Boys would help their fathers build neighborhood shrines. Girls would help their mothers decorate the shrines with flowers and offerings of fruit, vegetables, and lengths of home-made **linen.**

As well as the great temple and royal festivals, there were many local ones held at village and household shrines. These were to ensure that the family prospered, and the fields gave a good harvest. Priests used a special calendar based on the phases of the moon to work out when festivals should be held. Most followed the farmer's year, with celebrations to mark the plowing and sowing of the fields, and later the gathering of the crops.

Growing Up

▶◀▷▶◀▷▶◀▷▶◀▷▶◀▷▶◀▷▶◀▷▶◀▷▶◀▷▶◀▷▶◀▷▶◀▷▶◀▷▶◀▷

Boy to man

When ancient Egyptian boys were about 14 a priest performed a ceremony to show that they were now grown up. Children would also stop wearing the **sidelock** hairstyle around the age of 14. The **mummy** of a young prince, aged about 11, was found in the tomb of Pharaoh Amenhotep II.
The prince still wore a sidelock like a child.
This tells us that he had not yet reached adulthood.

This banquet scene is from the tomb of Ramses in Thebes. Only a rich family would have celebrated a marriage with such an event.

Girl to woman

As soon as girls were old enough to have children of their own
their family would begin to look for a husband for them. Marriage
was a matter for the people involved and their families. The bride
and bridegroom needed their parents' permission to get married,
and sometimes drew up a legal agreement to set out their rights as
husband and wife. This contract would be given to a third person,
or stored in a temple for safe-keeping. The couple might live
together for a year to see if the wife could have a baby. If the
couple got divorced because there was no baby, the wife had a
right to some of the property they had owned while they
were together.

Egyptians had no wedding ceremony, and no special clothes or
ring. The bride did not change her name. There was a noisy, happy
procession of well-wishers to accompany the bride from her family
home to the home of her new husband. Egyptians loved to have a
party, so there would have been a banquet as well. The groom
gave the bride a small gift of cash and corn to show that he would
provide for her. The bride's father often gave the newlyweds
household goods and food. Surviving statues of married couples
holding hands and accompanied by their children show that
husbands and wives felt affection for each other, and pride in their
sons and daughters. Because many women died in childbirth and
older husbands often died before their wives, there were many
single-parent families. Remarriage was common, so many children
had a stepfather or stepmother.

Treasures of a Boy King

When wealthy Egyptians died their tombs were filled with goods for them to use in the **afterlife.** Because royal tombs contained the finest things they were a target for tomb-robbers. When modern **archaeologists** began to **excavate** tombs they were disappointed to find that all the royal ones had been robbed of their contents.

Then, in 1922, English archaeologist Howard Carter discovered the tomb of Tutankhamen, a teenage pharaoh who had ruled for less than ten years around 1330 B.C.E. His tomb had been forgotten because it had been covered up by a deep layer of rock chips made during the building of neighboring tombs. Tutankhamen's tomb had been partly robbed twice, but sealed up again. It still contained his body, his gold coffins, gold funeral mask, and many treasures in excellent condition.

Inside the tomb

Tutankhamen's body was wrapped in fine bandages, with many charms and jewels between the different layers. The body was then sealed up in a coffin of solid gold, inside two outer coffins of wood covered with beaten gold. Around it in his burial chamber were four wooden **shrines,** covered with gold and religious writings. Other rooms in the tomb were crammed with

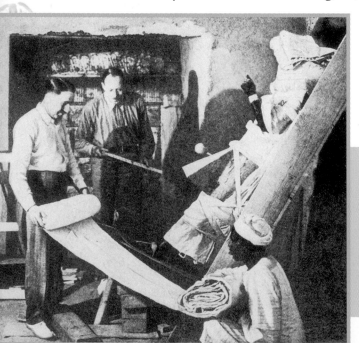

Howard Carter (left) was the English archaeologist to find the treasures of the tomb of Tutankhamen. Hidden from tomb robbers and located in the dry climate of Egypt, the coffins and mummy survived for hundreds of years.

clothes, a throne, three couches, food containers, statues, weapons, and six **chariots.** There were also model boats, a model granary, and dozens of wooden *shabti* dolls, intended to wait on the pharaoh as his servants in the afterlife. The **mummies** of two female children were buried with him. They were almost certainly his children that had not survived.

Because he was so young Tutankhamen probably had very little personal power. All the important decisions were made by his chief adviser, an old court official called Ay, and his top general Horemheb. Both ruled as pharaohs after Tutankhamen's early death. The survival of the boy king's tomb and treasures has made him the most famous pharaoh of all. However, he seems to have done little in his own short life to deserve such great fame.

The golden funeral-mask of the boy pharaoh Tutankhamen was found in the inner coffin. The boy is dressed as Osiris, god of the dead. He wears a blue and gold headcloth, a ceremonial beard, and images of a vulture and a cobra on his forehead.

How Do We Know?

▶◀▶ ◀▶ ◀▶ ◀▶ ◀▶ ◀▶ ◀▶ ◀▶ ◀▶ ◀▶ ◀▶ ◀▶ ◀▶ ◀▶ ◀▶ ◀◀

The key to unlocking Egypt's past was the discovery of a public notice, known as the Rosetta Stone, in 1799. This had an **inscription** carved on it in Greek, in a form of **hieratic** known as **demotic,** and also in **hieroglyphs.** Until the discovery of the Rosetta Stone, no one knew how to read hieroglyphs. It took almost thirty years for scholars to work out how to interpret the hieroglyphs. Once this was done they could read the thousands of other Egyptian inscriptions and documents surviving from the past.

Discoveries can also be made by re-examining what we already have. The pleated garment referred to on page 15 was part of a bundle of rags that Sir Flinders Petrie brought back to England from excavations in Egypt in 1912. No one realized what it was until it was re-examined in 1977.

These tombs and chapels were built by the people of Deir el-Medina. They left food and drink inside, hoping to sustain their ancestors, in the afterlife.

Nakht the weaver

New scientific methods help archaeologists learn more from a **mummy** than they could in the past. In 1974, a team examined the body of a teenage **weaver** called Nakht who lived during the reign of Ramses III (about 1187 B.C.E. to 1156 B.C.E.). The way his leg bones developed show that he had worked for long hours in a cross-legged position. The tapeworm found in his stomach suggests he ate meat. The red **granite** dust in his lungs showed he lived near Aswan, the only place in Egypt where this stone is found. He probably died of a lung disease or stomach infection, or a combination of the two. Although his family could not afford to have him **mummified** properly, they had stuffed his body with two shirts to keep its shape, and wrapped it in a **burial cloth.** Nakht's short life seems to have been like that of many children in ancient Egypt. It was filled with hard work, and troubled by some pain but also remembered by his family with love.

Even after two centuries of excavations much remains to be uncovered. So far archaeologists have concentrated on temples and the tombs of the great Egyptians. The workmen's village of Deir el-Medina has revealed a very different side to life from what can be learned from Tutankhamen's tomb. At Deir el-Medina the homes and belongings of workers and their families have been discovered. We do not yet know how typical that settlement was. The many unexcavated possibilities for the future include looking under known sites, under modern cities, in the marshy Nile delta, and in Egypt's thousands of villages and small towns.

Made of wood, this paddle shaped doll would have been the toy of an ancient Egyptian child about 4,000 years ago.

Timeline

All the following dates are B.C.E.:

Before 5000
Early settlers farm and build towns along the Nile.

About 3000
Menes unites Lower and Upper Egypt.

2575 to 2130 (The Old Kingdom)
The Great Pyramids are built at Giza. Trading expeditions and the war with the Libyans occur.

2130 to 1938
This is a time of weak rulers.

1938 to 1600 (The Middle Kingdom)
The power of the pharaohs is restored.

1630 to 1540
The invasion of Hyksos takes place. Egyptians face **chariots** for the first time.

1539 to 1075 (The New Kingdom)
Egypt's power is at its height. Akhenaten (Amenhotep IV) reigns in the 1300s. Tutankhamen (1333 to 1323), the boy-pharaoh whose tomb later reveals much about Egyptian life, lives and rules during this time. Ramses II (1279 to 1213), known as Ramses the Great, rules Egypt.

1075 to 665
Pharaohs of Libyan heritage rule Egypt. A dynasty of Kushite rulers gains power and rules during this time.

664 to 31
Local rulers struggle for power. Persian kings who did not rule Egypt, but styled themselves as pharaohs, come to power. Native rulers take power back from the Persians. In 332, Alexander the Great from Greece conquers the country. A new dynasty, under Ptolemy, a Greek, is founded in 305.

In 51, Cleopatra becomes joint ruler of Egypt with her brother. She rules alone from 47 until 31, when the Roman fleet defeats Egypt at the Battle of Actium. The Romans make Egypt a Roman province.

More Books to Read

▶ ◀ ▶ ◀ ▶ ◀ ▶ ◀ ▶ ◀ ▶ ◀ ▶ ◀ ▶ ◀ ▶ ◀ ▶ ◀ ▶ ◀ ▶ ◀ ▶ ◀ ▶ ◀ ▶ ◀ ▶ ◀

Barron's Educational Editorial Staff. *Egyptian Life*. Hauppage, N.Y.: Barron's Educational Series, Inc., 1998.

Harris, Geraldine and Delia Pemberton. *Illustrated Encyclopedia of Ancient Egypt*. Columbus, Ohio: McGraw-Hill Children's Publishing, 2000.

Hart, George. *Eyewitness: Ancient Egypt*. New York: DK Publishing, 2001.

Nicholson, Robert. *Ancient Egypt*. Broomall, Penn.: Chelsea House Publishers, 1994.

Quie, Sarah. *Myths and Civilization of the Ancient Egyptians*. Columbus, Ohio: McGraw-Hill Children's Publishing, 2000.

Rosati, A. *The Atlas of Ancient Egypt*. Columbus, Ohio: McGraw-Hill Children's Publishing, 2000.

Shuter, Jane. *Valley of the Kings*. Chicago: Heinemann Library, 1999.

Glossary

afterlife life after death

amulet lucky charm

ancestor family member from long ago

archaeologist person who studies ancient objects to understand the past

bronze metal made by mixing tin and copper

burial cloth cloth used to wrap a dead body

chariot two-wheeled cart used for racing or warfare

civilization developed society

copper reddish-gold colored metal used for tools, weapons, beads or bangles

delta river mouth split into smaller streams divided by islands

demotic simplified version of writing

dynasty ruling family

dysentery stomach infection causing the sufferer to go to the toilet often

epidemic large-scale outbreak of a disease

excavate dig up items from the past

flax plant whose fibers can be made into linen cloth

granite very hard kind of stone

hieratic shortened hieroglyphs use by priests

hieroglyphs symbols used for Egyptian writing

historian person who studies ancient documents to understand the past

inscription writing carved into a surface

irrigation ditch/canal channel dug to carry water to or from a field

kilt wrap-around, knee-length skirt

linen light cloth woven from fibers of the flax plant

loincloth garment worn around the middle like shorts

midwife nurse who helps women to have babies

mummify to preserve a dead body as a mummy

mummy body preserved by removing internal parts, drying flesh with chemicals, and then bandaging in layers

New Kingdom period from the 16th to the 11th century B.C.E.

papyrus paper made from the spongy tissue of a reed plant

quarterstaff long, thick stick used for fighting

serf farmer who is not free to leave his village

shrine place where gods are worshiped

sidelock bunch of hair hanging from one side of the head

slave servant owned by his or her employer

tunic sleeveless knee-length garment, often pulled in at the waist

weaver person who uses a loom to turn yarn into cloth

wet nurse servant who feeds babies with her breast-milk

will written document listing who should get what from a dead person's property

Index